EDITOR: LEE JOHNSON

OSPREY
MILITARY

NEW VANGUAR

STURMGESCHUTZ

ASSAULT GUN 1940-42

Text by
HILARY DOYLE & TOM JENTZ
Colour plates by
PETER SARSON

First published in Great Britain in 1996 by
Osprey, an imprint of Reed Consumer Books Ltd.
Michelin House, 81 Fulham Road,
London SW3 6RB
and Auckland, Melbourne, Singapore and Toronto

ISBN 1 85532 537 3

Filmset by KDI, Newton le Willows
Printed through Worldprint Ltd, Hong Kong

Designed by Paul Kime
Edited by Denis Baldry
Series editor Iain MacGregor

Artist's Note

Readers may care to note the original paintings from which
the colour plates in this book were prepared are available
for private sale. All reproduction copyright whatsoever is
retained by the publisher. All enquiries should be
addressed to:

Peter Sarson
46 Robert-Louis Stevenson Avenue
Westbourne
Bournemouth
Dorset BH4 8EJ

The publishers regret that they can enter into no corre-
spondence upon this matter.

Editor's note

Readers may wish to read this title in conjunction with the
following Osprey titles:

DESIGN AND DEVELOPMENT

In 1936 Manstein drafted the fundamental tactics for the Sturmartillerie (assault artillery). Batteries of six guns were to be assigned to infantry divisions. These were to be the motorised equivalent of the elite light artillery batteries from World War I, but possessing the advantage of armour protection. With the exception of the copycat Italian Semovente and the Hungarian Zrinyi, a similar armoured vehicle (a light artillery piece with limited traverse mounted in a well armoured self-propelled chassis of low silhouette), was not produced by any other country during World War II. The tank advocates (especially Guderian) have always contended that a tank (possessing turret armament traversable through 360°) can be employed as a Sturmgeschütz, but a Sturmgeschütz cannot fight as a tank. One only has to look at the kill ratios against tanks achieved by the low profile Sturmgeschütz with the short-barrelled gun to observe that those advocating the use of tanks for both purposes paid heavily for their preference.

Design specifications

On 15 June 1936, In 4 (Inspektorat des Artillerie) authorised the Heeres Waffenamt (army ordnance department) to design an armoured vehicle to support infantry in accordance with the following specifications:

i   Mount a gun with a calibre of at least 75 mm.
ii If possible, the traverse arc of the gun was to exceed 30°.
iii The elevation of the gun was to be sufficient to achieve a range of 6000 m.
iv The armour penetration capability of the gun was to be sufficient to defeat all known armour thicknesses at a range of 500 m (ie, 40 mm on the French tanks).
v   All round armour protection was required. The top of the superstructure was to be open without a turret. The frontal armour (when placed at an angle of 30° from vertical) was to be proof against 2 cm armour piercing rounds. The side and rear were to be proof against 7.92 mm steel-cored armour piercing rounds fired from rifles or machine guns.
vi The total height of the vehicle was not to exceed the height of a standing man.
vii The remaining measurements were to be based on the size of the tank chassis that was utilised.

Development history

The Heeres Waffenamt awarded the contract for detailed design of the chassis and superstructure to Daimler-Benz and the contract for detailed design of gun to Krupp. Previously, Daimler-Benz had been awarded the detailed design contracts for the Pz.Kpfw.III chassis, which was also selected for this application.

As recorded in Krupp's annual business report for fiscal year 1935/36, they had received contracts to design the '7,5 cm Geschütz L/24 für Sturmartillerie (Selbstfahrlafette)' (75 mm gun of 24 calibre length for self-propelled assault artillery). Krupp was to provide one experimental gun for the price of 24,000 Reichsmarks as well as four wooden models of the gun for 6,000 Reichsmarks.

On 15 December 1936, the Sturmartillerie was referred to by the codename of 'Pak(Sfl.)' (self-propelled anti-tank gun). This name was modified to 'Pz.Sfl.III (s.Pak)' (third model of armoured self-propelled heavy anti-tank gun) in 1937.

The operational experimental gun and the four

wooden models were to be mounted in five chassis appropriated from the Pz.Kpfw.III Ausf.B series produced by Daimler-Benz. Krupp's contract was subsequently expanded to five experimental guns which were delivered in 1938. The five vehicles in this 'Versuchsserie' (experimental series), completed in 1938, were used to perfect the design and establish the basic tactical doctrine. Due to their soft steel superstructures, they were not employable in combat. But they remained in use for crew training at least throughout 1941.

As originally designed, the top of the 's.Pak' was open without a roof. In 1936, an open top was considered to have significant tactical advantages. In comparison to the crew in a tank, the crew of an open-topped armoured vehicle could easily spot targets and be able to hear approaching vehicles.

In 1939, the decision was made to enclose the fighting compartment with a roof. The reason given was that tactical requirements had changed. The nature of this tactical change was not specified in the original report. The need for a roof may have been caused by concern that small arms fire would ricochet off the inside of the walls when the vehicle was on a slope. There was a very low probability of mortar or artillery rounds hitting the top of moving or even stationary 's.Pak'.

The thin roof plates offered insufficient protection against direct hits from 81 mm mortar, 75 mm high explosive artillery shells, or any larger shells. A wire-mesh screen was considered to be an adequate deterrent to hand grenades at the time. Since the roof was far from leak proof, it was not designed to prevent the ignited contents of Molotov cocktails from seeping into the fighting compartment.

After the roof had been initially designed, delays in its manufacture occurred when the troops requested that it be modified for indirect fire. A hatch was cut into the roof so that an artillery panoramic gun sight could be mounted with its head protruding above the roof line. This panoramic gun sight was used to sight at aiming stakes (instead of at the target). Commands from the battery fire control centre informed the gunner of the angle to set in order to engage a target. In this way targets could be engaged by 'indirect fire' (without the gunner aiming directly at the target).

Official designations

On 7 February 1940, the name was officially changed from 's.Pak' to '7,5 cm Kanone (Pz.Sfl.)' (armoured self-propelled 75 mm gun). Shortly thereafter on 28 March 1940, the name was

Above; A Sturmgeschütz Ausf.E. during training exercises. The 9mm superstructure side plates, as had been previously seen on the models Ausf. A-D., were replaced by angled 30 mm plated side walls within the superstructure itself. (Author)

changed from 7,5 cm Kanone (Pz.Sfl.) to 'Sturmgeschütz' (assault gun), a designation it would retain throughout the rest of the war. The full official designation printed on the serial number plates and used in manuals was 'gepanzerte Selbstfahrlafette für Sturmgeschütz 7,5 cm Kanone (Sd.Kfz.142)', which was abbreviated to gp.Sfl.f.Stu.G. 7,5 cm K. (Sd.Kfz.142).

General description

The chassis design for the first production series was based on the '5.Serie/Z.W.' design (also known as the Pz.Kpfw.III Ausf.E). The component parts of the chassis specifically designed for the first Sturmgeschütz production series was the hull armour (with drawing/part number 021St33901); hydraulic assisted steering (021St33932); driver's seat (021St33933); brake ventilation (021St33934); track brakes (021St33937); and the final drives (021St33938 &

Rear of one of the Versuchsserie based on the early Pz.Kpfw.III Ausf.B chassis during a training exercise in 1940. The ammunition is being loaded into the 's. Pak' from the specially-built semi-track ammunition carrier Sd.Kfz.252. (Author)

A crewman jumps from one of the 's. Pak' Versuchsserie during training at Jüterbog. Note the inspection hatches in the front hull armour of the Pz.Kpfw.III Ausf.B chassis and the differences in the design of the armour surrounding the gun. (Author)

39). The rest of the component parts remained unchanged from the 5.Serie/Z.W. design with drawing/part numbers in the series 021St9203 through 021St9253. Armour protection consisted of the 50 mm thick driver's front plate at an angle from the vertical of 9°, 50 mm hull front at 20° and 50°, 30 mm superstructure and hull sides at 0°, 30 mm tail plates at 10° and 30°, 10 mm fighting compartment roof at 77-90°, 16 mm rear deck at 80-87°, and 15 mm belly plate at 90°. The large gun mantlet and the armour cover plate for the gun's recoil and recuperator cylinders were both 50 mm thick. In addition, 8 mm thick plates sloping at 30° were added as an afterthought along the superstructure sides. These were mounted at a time long before consideration was given to protection against armour-defeating rounds based on the hollow charge principle. Therefore, they must have been introduced as spaced armour to defeat the tungsten cored projectiles that Germany knew the French were using as early as 1936. The armour specifications for the initial production series consisted of all homogeneous plates.

Hatches were provided in the hull roof directly above the gunner's, loader's and commander's positions. The driver was expected to escape through the steering brake inspection hatch in the glacis plate. The twin hatch covers were of equal size, hinged to the sides (instead of the front and rear as on the Pz.Kpfw.III).

The driver had a visor mounted in the front plate. When closed for added protection, he could use the KFF.2 twin periscopes. A fixed vision slit was mounted to the driver's left in the superstructure wall but he had no view at all to the right side. The gunner's only view was provided by the Sfl.Z.F periscopic gun sight with an aperture in the superstructure front. The view to the sides was extremely limited due to the armour sides for the sight aperture. The commander was provided with a SF.14Z scissors periscope that projected through the opened hatch when in use. When not

The first Sturmgeschütz Ausf.A was delivered by Daimler-Benz Werk 40 in Berlin in January 1940. This front three-quarter view clearly shows the narrow track and wheels. The entire order for 30 Ausf.A in the 1.Serie had been produced by June 1940. (National Archives)

Left side view of the Sturmgeschütz Ausf.A. (National Archives)

Three-quarter rear view of the Sturmgeschütz Ausf.A. (National Archives)

Right side view of the Sturmgeschütz Ausf.A. (National Archives)

One of the Sturmgeschütz Ausf.A of 16 SturmBatterie/ Infantrie-Regiment 'Gross-Deutschland' during the campaign in France 1940. This unit took delivery of the first six Ausf.A's. Note the mixture of narrow and wide wheels.

in use, the SF.14Z mount was folded down and the binoculars strapped to the left wall. No vision devices were provided for the loader. Overall therefore the crew's vision was very restricted when they buttoned up.

The commander's seat was spring loaded and adjustable in height. It could be locked in position by a foot pedal. This enabled him to look out over the roof in the raised position or to observe under cover with the scissors periscope in the lowered position. The loader's seat was hinged on the right wall so that it could fold up out of the way. The gunner's seat was attached to the gun mount.

The main armament consisted of the 7,5 cm Kanone L/24 (75 mm gun, 24 calibres long), that had been adapted from the 7,5 cm Kw.K. L/24 (tank gun) originally designed for the Pz.Kpfw.IV. As with the tank gun, it had a semi-automatic vertical sliding breech and electric primer firing. It had the same gun tube and chambered the same ammunition as the tank gun, but similarities stopped there.

The mounting consisted of a heavy rectangular frame carrying the gun trunnions, the gun mantelet, and the cradle. The gun could be elevated manually by hand through an arc from -10° to +20° and traversed by hand 12° to the right and left of centre.

A total of 44 rounds for the main gun was stowed in sheet metal bins with hinged lids and quick release clips. A total of 32 rounds were stowed in front of the loader to the right of the gun. The other 12 were stowed in a bin mounted on the rear wall of the fighting compartment.

In addition to the main armament, the crew was provided with two machine pistols, each with 192 rounds of ammunition. Twelve stick hand grenades were also carried in clips along the rear ammunition bin. A smoke candle rack was mounted on the upper tail plate. The five smoke candles could be remotely released one at a time from inside the fighting compartment.

Originally, the Sturmgeschütz was only outfitted with one ultra-short wave receiving radio set without intercom. Only the commander had head phones. As in a normal towed artillery application, a loud speaker was used for the gun crew to hear the commands. This loud speaker was mounted to the left front of the gunner. The commander communicated with the driver utilising a speaking tube with funnels at each end.

Power was delivered to the tracks by a drive train consisting of a high performance Maybach HL 120 TRM 12-cylinder petrol (US = gasoline) engine delivering 265 metric hp at 2,600 rpm, through a ten-speed Maybach Variorex SRG 328 145 transmission, onto the planetary gear steering and final drives to the drive sprockets. The combat weight of 20.7 metric tons was distributed over six sets of 520 mm diameter rubber-tyred

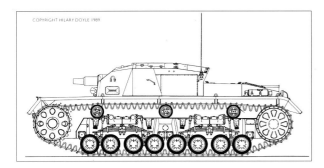

1:76 scale side view of a Versuchsserie 's.Pak' (Author)

twin roadwheels per side sprung by single transverse torsion bars. The unlubricated Kgs 6111/380/120 track (360 mm wide track with 380 mm long track pins) provided a relatively high ground pressure of 0.9 kg/cm².

PRODUCTION MODIFICATIONS

As was the practice with every German armoured vehicle with a long production run, modifications were introduced before completion of each Ausführung. It would therefore be incorrect to expect that all of the Sturmgeschütz of the same Ausführung (model) looked exactly alike. But with the exception of the Sturmgeschütz Ausf.C and D whose external appearances were identical, each Ausführung had distinctive identifying characteristics.

Sturmgeschütz Ausf.A, Fgst.Nr. 90001-90030
The normal transmission for the Pz.Kpfw.III was originally intended to be mounted in the Sturmgeschütz. But when it came to fitting the transmission in the first Sturmgeschütz it quickly became apparent that the housing had to be altered due to interference with the base of the gun mount. The modified Maybach Variorex SRG 328 145 transmission for the Sturmgeschütz was designated as drawing/part number 021St33940.

During the production run the Notek lights were mounted on the left track guard, the hooded headlight at the front and the double split tail lights at the rear. The tail lights were designed for maintaining the proper distance in convoys at night.

If the following driver saw four lights he was too close, two lights he was correct, and one light he was too far back. Due to the unacceptable wear of the narrower (520 x 75 - 397) rubber tyres, wider tyres (520 x 95 - 397) were introduced. The rims for the roadwheels were extended by tack welding an extra ring to the outside to support the wider tyre, but it still retained the original part number (021St9205).

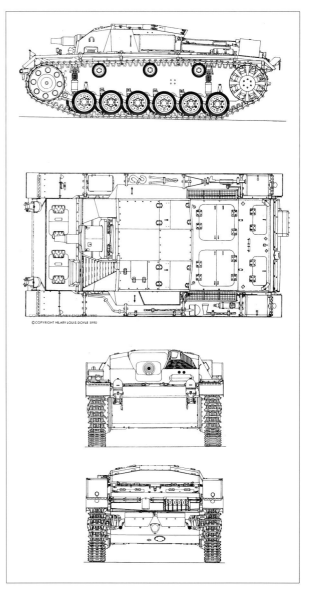

1:76 scale drawings of a Sturmgeschütz Ausf.A. The wheels are of the narrow type to suit 38 cm track. (Author)

Sturmgeschütz Ausf.A, Fgst.Nr. 90401-90420

For reasons that have yet to be discovered from original documents, during the period from June through September 1940, 20 Sturmgeschütz were produced using normal 6.Serie/Z.W. (Pz Kpfw III Ausf.G) chassis. Their superstructures had the hatch configuration above the gunner associated with a design change for the Sturmgeschütz Ausf.B roof.

During this period, the frontal armour plates on PzKpfw III hulls were still only 30 mm thick. To increase frontal armour protection up to the standard for a Sturmgeschütz, the converted hulls were reinforced with an additional 20 mm thick armour plate bolted to the front nose plate.

This series of Sturmgeschütz retained the standard PzKpfw III Ausf.G characteristics, including the escape hatches on the hull sides, the two steering brake maintenance hatches in the glacis plate (hinged to the front and rear), and the two vent cowlings on the upper nose plate for providing cooling air to the steering brakes. A hinge for the left maintenance hatch in the glacis interfered with mounting a shot deflector on the glacis plate for the driver's visor. The armoured cover design (hinged at the top), for the inertial crank starter-

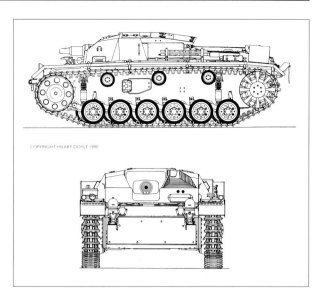

1:76 scale drawings of a Sturmgeschütz Ausf.A. (Fgst.Nr. 90401-420) with the chassis of the PzKpfw III Ausf.G. (Author)

port in the upper rear hull, was introduced with the PzKpfw III Ausf.G. The running gear was still configured for the narrower Kgs 6111/380/120 track links but had the 95 mm wide rubber tyres.

As revealed in the official parts manual for the 'Fahrgestell Sturmgeschütz (75 mm) (SdKfz 142)' dated February 1944, these 20 Sturmgeschütz were designated as Ausf.A and assigned chassis numbers in the 90401 to 90500 range. The Ausf.A designation was correctly applied because these converted PzKpfw III chassis still possessed the ten-speed Maybach SRG 328 145 transmission.

Sturmgeschütz Ausf.B, Fgst.Nr.90101-90350 and 90501-90550

The second production series ordered for the Sturmgeschütz adopted the automotive improvements initiated for the 7.Serie/Z.W. (PzKpfw III Ausf.H) chassis design. The modified components included those associated with the wider track, including the roadwheel arm (021St39002); return rollers (021St39007); 10 mm inside and 30 mm outside spacers installed for sprockets on the drive wheels; and the Kgs 61/400/120 (380 mm wide track with 400 mm long track pins) track (021St39010). The foremost return rollers on both sides were mounted further forward to prevent

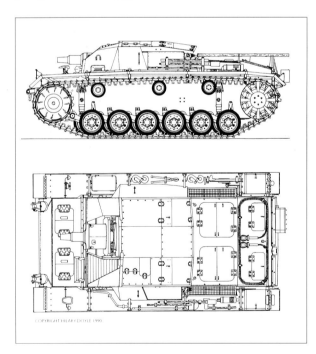

1:76 scale drawings of a Sturmgeschütz Ausf.B with the new cast sprocket for the 40 cm track. (Author)

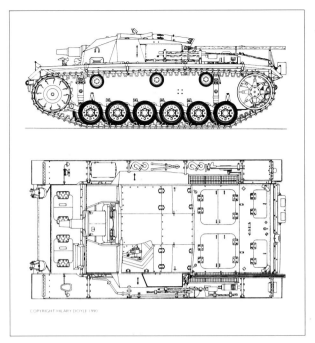

1:76 scale drawings of a Sturmgeschütz Ausf.C. (Author)

77 transmission, the clutch was attached to the fly wheel for the Maybach HL 120 TRM engine. Externally, the track guards (021St39042 & 43) rear fender flaps and the exhaust mufflers were changed. Component parts for the chassis specifically designed for the Sturmgeschütz Ausf.B included the hull armour (021St33951) and the hydraulically-assisted steering (021St33960). The rest of the component parts for the chassis remained unchanged from the Ausf.A.

The superstructure remained largely unchanged. The hatches over the gun sight and the gunner were redesigned. The forward hatch for the gun sight was lengthened and mounted with two hinges. The gunner's hatch was narrower and mounted with a single side hinge.

During the production run cast drive wheels (021St39008) were introduced and an armour cover was mounted over the smoke candle rack on the upper rear hull. By the autumn of 1940, the large stowage boxes were no longer mounted on the track guards. Starting with Fgst.Nr. 90321, a removable guard around the clutch housing was installed on the firewall.

Sturmgeschütz Ausf.C, Fgst.Nr.90551-90600

The main change incorporated into the Ausf.C was the new periscopic SflZF 1 gunsight (drawing/part number 021St33979) with the associated modification of the roof hatch. The right side of the single large hatch over the gunner was cut away to allow the head of the periscopic gun sight to protrude above the roof. The forward sloping roof of the superstructure was also modified on both sides and the direct sight port in the left

sagging track from slapping and catching on the underside of the track guards when starting and also to reduce the incidents of thrown track.

Internally, the modifications included the steering gear (021St39012); SSG 77 synchronised six-speed transmission (021St39013); ventilation for brakes (021St39018); and track brakes (021St39045). With the introduction of the SSG

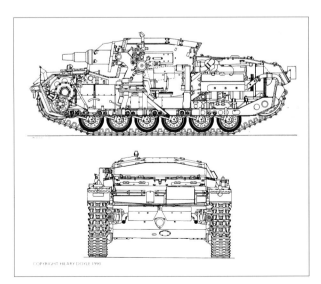

1:76 scale drawings of a Sturmgeschütz Ausf.D. (Author)

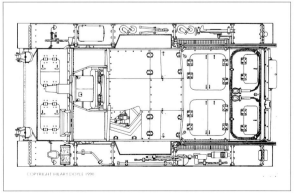

1:76 scale plan view of a Sturmgeschütz Ausf.E. (Author)

A Sturmgeschütz Ausf.B passing a Luftwaffe unit in Russia. (Bundesarchiv 348 1142 3a)

superstructure front was deleted. The only component part of the chassis that was specifically modified for the Sturmgeschütz Ausf.C was the hull armour (021St33973). This was a minor change associated with mounting seals around the steering brake access hatches (021St33973-1). Two component parts modified for the 7.Serie/Z.W. (PzKpfw III Ausf.H) that were first introduced with the Sturmgeschütz Ausf.C (instead of the Ausf.B) were the idler wheel (021St39004) and the oil bath engine air filters (021St39080). The rest of the component parts for the chassis remained unchanged from the Ausf.B.

During the production run of the Sturmgeschütz Ausf.C, the locks for the steering brake access hatches were changed from a single lock using a skeleton key (covered by hinged rectangular box shaped cover) to two locks using a centimetre square drift key (021St33974).

Sturmgeschütz Ausf.D, Fgst.Nr.90601-90750

The only component parts identified in the detailed parts manual that were modified specifically for the Sturmgeschütz Ausf.D chassis was the hull armour (021St33978) and an electric bell (021St2304) mounted near the driver's right ear for the commander to signal the driver. Because no other changes were identified in the detailed parts manual, the modification to the hull armour may have been associated with the Ausf.D, which was the first series to feature face-hardened frontal armour. The rest of the component parts for the chassis remained unchanged from the Ausf.C.

Sturmgeschütz destined for southern Russia, Greece, and North Africa were modified for 'tropical' employment while still at the assembly plant. Fan speed was increased and armoured covers were mounted over holes cut into the rear deck hatches to improve the flow of air into and out of the engine compartment.

Sturmgeschütz Ausf.E, Fgst.Nr.90751-91034

Component parts of the chassis specifically designed for the Sturmgeschütz Ausf.E included reduced size hinges for the steering brake access hatches which slightly modified the hull armour

Table 1: Sturmgeschütz production history

Date	Number Produced Monthly	Number Delivered for Issue	Fgst.Nr. Attained	Notes:
1940				
Jan	1	0	90001	*Ausf.A Fgst.Nr.*
Feb	3	1	90004	*90001-90030 and*
Mar	6	0	90010	*90401-90420*
Apr	10	14	90020	
May	10	10	90030	
Jun	12	12	90412	
Jul	22	22	90114	*Ausf.B Fgst.Nr.*
Aug	20	22	90134	*90101-90350 and*
Sep	29	22	90163	*90501-90550*
Oct	35	20	90198	
Nov	35	25	90233	
Dec	29	31	90262	
1941				
Jan	36	43	90298	
Feb	30	29	90328	
Mar	30	36	90508	*Ausf.C Fgst.Nr.*
Apr	47	26	90555	*90551-90600*
May	48	60	90603	*Ausf.D Fgst.Nr.*
Jun	56	42	90659	*90601-90750*
Jul	34	56	90693	
Aug	50	44	90743	
Sep	38	41	90781	*Ausf.E Fgst.Nr.*
Oct	71	81	90852	*90751-91034*
Nov	46	42	90898	
Dec	46	46	90944	
1942				
Jan	45	33	90989	
Feb	45	30	91034	*Last Ausf.E*
Mar	0	23		

(021St33982) as well as the hatch covers (021St33982-1). The track guards (021St33991) were redesigned to fit the new superstructure side panniers. The rest of the component parts for the chassis remained unchanged from the Ausf.D.

The major improvement in the Ausf.E was the lengthening of the left armoured pannier and the addition of an armoured pannier on the right side of the superstructure. Both the right and left superstructure panniers were now longer than the single one on the left side of the previous Ausf. This modification came about because of a change in tactics. Instead of using a half-tracked armoured observation vehicle SdKfz 253, platoon leaders and battery commanders were using Sturmgeschütz as command vehicles.

Consequently, additional space was needed for mounting the transmitting and receiving radio sets. When assigned to a commander, the Sturmgeschütz was outfitted with both an ultra short wave FuG15 receiver set with transformer in the left pannier and an ultra short wave FuG16 10 watt transmitter and receiver sets with transformer in the right pannier. The FuG16 was operated by the loader.

Space was also available in the left-hand pannier to store an additional six rounds of ammunition for the main gun. The 8 mm slanted armour plates, mounted on the superstructure sides of previous models, were discontinued.

The Sturmgeschütz Ausf.E was the last of the Sturmgeschütz series to be produced with the 75

The second series of Sturmgeschütz Ausf.A was, for some unknown reason, built on the chassis of the Pz.Kpfw.III Ausf.G. As the frontal armour on the exisiting Pz.Kpfw.III was only 30 mm thick, an additional 20 mm plate was bolted on to create a 50 mm front. This series may be identified by the armoured air intake covers on the upper nose plate and the hull side escape hatch. (Karl Heinz Munch)

mm Kanone L/24.

Retrofitted modifications

In the official stowage plan D652/46 dated 1 March 1941, each Sturmgeschütz was to be outfitted with an FuG16 radio with both a transmitter and receiver set, a single set of earphones, and a loud speaker. The transmitter was mounted to the right of the commander's seat on the rear wall of the fighting compartment. When the

Sturmgeschütz was issued to a platoon leader or battery commander a second receiver set (FuG15) was mounted to the right of the transmitter on the rear wall of the fighting compartment. There was no intercom set. Communication with the driver was with the speaking tube or (starting with the Ausf.D) a signal bell.

There were very few general orders that authorised field modifications to the Sturmgeschütz in any way. In a general order published on 7 June 1941, each of the seven Sturmgeschütz in each battery was authorised to carry an MG 34 machine gun with 600 rounds of ammunition. The Sturmgeschütz was not provided with a mount or gun shield for the MG 34. To bring the MG 34 into action, the loader was exposed above his opened hatch.

A general order dated 20 September 1941 authorised the units to modify Sturmgeschütz Fgst.Nr.90101–90320 by replacing the guard welded to the firewall that covered the clutch housing with a removable guard.

General order dated 20 December 1941 authorised the following modifications: (1) weld a bar onto the lower front hull to hold 11 spare track links; (2) fasten curved sheet metal deflectors to redirect the exhausted cooling air at the rear of Sturmgeschütz (Sd.Kfz.142) Ausf.A to E; and (3) mount two spare wheels on the fenders of Sturmgeschütz (Sd.Kfz.142) Ausf.A to E.

A general order dated 30 January 1942, authorised a modification for those Sturmgeschütz used in 'tropical' areas. In order to avoid dust damaging the engines, intake air was drawn from the fighting

	K.Gr.rot Pz.	Gr.38 HL	Gr.38 HL/A	Gr.38 HL/B
Table 2: Armour penetration performance				
Shell weight:	6.8 kg	4.5 kg	4.4 kg	4.57 kg
Initial velocity:	385 m/s	452 m/s	450 m/s	450 m/s
Range:				
100 m	41 mm	45 mm	70 mm	75 mm
500 m	39 mm	45 mm	70 mm	75 mm
1000 m	35 mm	45 mm	70 mm	75 mm
1500 m	33 mm	45 mm	70 mm	75 mm

Table 3: Accuracy

Ammunition:	K.Gr.rot Pz.		Gr.38 HL	
Range:	Tests	Practice	Tests	Practice
100 m	100	100	100	100
500 m	100	100	100	99
1000 m	98	73	92	60
1500 m	74	38	61	26

compartment as a prefilter to the normal air filters.

General order dated 7 April 1942 authorised a heater made by installing ductwork and louvers to direct air warmed by the radiators into the crew compartment.

PRODUCTION HISTORY

In addition to designing the chassis and super-structure, Daimler-Benz was awarded the contract for assembly of the first series of 30 Sturmgeschütz. The first Ausf.A was to be completed in December 1939 and the series completed in April 1940. Due to a series of problems, production was delayed by a month, resulting in only four batteries being sent into France in May and June of 1940.

Assembly contracts for the second and subsequent series of Sturmgeschütz were awarded to Alkett. For reasons unclear in the original documents, a short series of 20 additional Ausf.A – produced using Pz.Kpfw.III Ausf.G chassis – was inserted between the production of the 1.Serie (30 Ausf.A) and 2.Serie (250 Ausf.B).

The small contracts for extra Sturmgeschütz, in units of 50 additional Ausf.B and only 50 Ausf.C, show that there was no long term commitment to this production programme in early 1940. Following proof of their value in France, contracts were placed for 150 Ausf.D followed by a larger order for 500 Ausf.E. Only 284 of this contract

were completed as Ausf.E, the balance being assembled with the longer 7.5 cm StuK 40 gun and designated as Ausf.F. As shown in Table 1, Production History, the dip in production that occurred in September 1941 was due a shortage created by shipping a large number of replacement Maybach HL 120 TRM engines to the Eastern Front. As can be seen the shortage was made good by the following month.

CAPABILITIES

Operational characteristics demonstrate the effectiveness of an armoured fighting vehicle by relating its capabilities to effectively deliver firepower, manoeuvre, and survive on the battlefield.

Firepower

The effectiveness of firepower from the main gun is dependent upon the penetration ability of the armour piercing rounds, inherent accuracy of the gun, characteristics of the gun sights, and ability to get quickly and accurately on target.

Penetration statistics for armour plate were expressed in terms of the thickness in mm that could be perforated when the plate was laid back at an angle from the vertical of 30°. The penetrating ability of AP rounds fired from the 75 mm Stu.K. L/24 was determined by tests conducted at firing ranges which proved that the results shown in Table 2 could be achieved.

Of the total ammunition load of 44 rounds, the recommended ratio was 12% K.Gr.rot Pz.

Sturmgeschütz Ausf.A, belonging to SS-Sturmbatterie of Leibstandarte SS Adolf Hitler. Originally these vehicles had been intended for Sturmbatterie 666 but were diverted to the SS unit instead. This unit saw service during the campaign in France where this photograph was taken. The key emblem of the LSSAH was painted in white on the starter cover on the motor compartment rear plate. A wolf's head was painted to the left of the starter cover. A small white point surrounded by a circle (representing the assignment of the Sturmbatterie to the II Bn.) was painted on the right and on the back of the rear stowage box.(Author)

(armour piercing, capped, ballistic capped with explosive filler and tracer), 65% Sprenggranaten (high explosive shells), and 23% Nebelgranaten (smoke shells). A fourth type of round was the Gr.38 HL (HEAT) based on the hollow charge principle. The Gr.38 HL was purpose-designed as an AP round with excellent fragmentation performance. It was carried in place of Sprenggranaten and used either to combat tanks or as an effective HE round against soft targets.

The original design of the Gr.38 HL was less accurate and was much less destructive after penetration than the K.Gr.rot Pz. Penetration performance was greatly increased with the Gr.38 HL/A and HL/B, improved versions of the HEAT rounds. A Sturmgeschütz Ausf.D was captured in North Africa in 1942 with 88 rounds on board of which 20 were hollow charge (Gr.38 HL/A) and 35 capped armour piercing shells (K.Gr.rot Pz).

Due to the high arcing flight of low velocity rounds fired from the 75 mm Stu.K. L/24, it could only be expected to hit vertical point targets such as tanks at fairly short ranges. The estimated accuracy is given as the probability (in percentage) of hitting a target measuring 2 x 2 m, representing the target presented by the front of an opposing tank.

These accuracy tables assume that the actual range to the target has been correctly determined and that the distribution of hits centred on the point of aim. The first column shows the accuracy obtained during controlled test firing of the gun to determine the pattern of dispersion. The second column includes the variation expected during practice firing due to differences between guns, ammunition, and gunners. As shown in Table 3, both columns were reported in the accuracy tables extracted from an original manual on the 75 mm Stu.K. L/24. These accuracy tables do not reflect the actual probability of hitting a target under battlefield conditions. Due to errors in estimating the range, the probability of any hit beyond 800 m was slight when firing these low velocity rounds with their associated high arcing trajectories.

The Sfl.ZF periscopic gun sight for the StuG

Table 4: Penetration performance of allied tank guns

	Russian 45 mm L/46 AP Shell 1.43 kg 760 m/s	Russian 76.2 mm L/41.5 AP Shell 7.6 kg 625 m/s	British 2-pdr AP Shot 2.08 lb 2,600 ft/s	American 37 mm M6 APC 1.92 lb 2600 ft/s	American 75 mm M2 AP Shot 14.72 lb 1850 ft/s
50 mm Super Front	100 m	2000+ m	200 yds	500 yds	600 yds
50 mm Hull Front	100 m	2000+ m	200 yds	600 yds	700 yds
30 mm Hull Side	1500 m	2000+ m	1500 yds	2000 yds	2000 yds
30 mm Hull Rear	1500 m	2000+ m	1500 yds	2000 yds	2000 yds

Ausf.A and B had an aperture in the superstructure front. The StuG Ausf.C, D and E had an improved Sfl.ZF1 periscopic gun sight with the head of the periscope extending through an aperture in the roof. The pattern in the gunsight reticle consisted of 7 triangles, separated by 4 mils. Placing the target on the point of a triangle allowed the gunner to aim without obstructing the view of the target. The distances between triangles were used to lead moving targets.

The triangle height and separation distances in mils were also used as an aid in estimating the range to a target. The range scale for the K.Gr.rot Pz. was graduated at 100-m intervals out to a range of 1500 m and the second range scale for the Sprenggranaten was graduated out to a range of 6000 m.

The 75 mm Stu.K. L/24 had a limited traverse of 12° to the left and 12° to the right of the centreline. The entire Sturmgeschütz had to be turned to engage targets outside of this limited arc of 24°.

Mobility

The ability of the Sturmgeschütz to negotiate

Rear view of one of the first Sturmgeschütz Ausf.B delivered to Sturmbatterie 667 on 12 September 1940. The old drive sprocket has been modified by fitting a spacer to accommodate the wider Kgs 61/400/120 track. (Bundesarchiv rot 79/67/8)

obstacles and cross difficult terrain is related by the performance characteristics listed in Plate D.

Survivability

The major asset of the Sturmgeschütz was its low profile and thick frontal armour. The side and rear armour protection was only sufficient to eliminate any threat from small calibre automatic weapons.

The six drawings (see page 24) extracted from a manual dated 2 February 1942 relate the ability of the Sturmgeschütz to defeat the opponents tanks considered to be difficult to combat. Other opposing tanks with armour protection up to 40 mm thick were easily defeated by the Sturmgeschütz at all normal combat ranges.

However the armour provided for this vehicle could be defeated by it's opponents' guns at the ranges shown in Table 4. The frontal armour provided adequate protection against the smaller cali-

A Sturmgeschütz Ausf.B of Sturmgeschütz-Abteilung 226 crosses a temporary bridge during the attack on Russia. The hatches in the roof for the gun sight have been modi- *fied but the main difference when compared to the Ausf.A is the new six-speed gearbox. (Bundesarchiv 347 1058 32)*

bre anti-tank and tank guns for which it was designed. The 50 mm face-hardened plates even proved effective against the 75 mm uncapped AP Shot fired by the M2 Gun in the American Lee/Grant. It was overmatched by the 76.2 mm armour piercing shells fired from the Russian T-34 and KV-I. But due to its extremely low profile, the Sturmgeschütz still presented a difficult target.

This Sturmgeschütz Ausf.B (Fgst.Nr. 90195) was built in October 1940. It was issued to Sturmgeschütz-Abteilung 197. (Spielberger)

OPERATIONAL HISTORY

Tactics

A manual entitled *Instructions for the Employment of Sturmartillerie* was first published in May 1940 with a second edited version being released in April 1942.

The second version was essentially similar in substance with the first, except that the second volume contains some additional information on advances in technology. Both these documents have been combined into one and any contradictions between the two versions are noted.

Basic principles and role

'The Sturmgeschütz (75 mm gun on an armoured self-propelled mount) is an offensive weapon. It can only fire in the general direction in which the vehicle is pointing (limited traverse of 24°). Owing to its cross-country performance and its armour, it is able to follow its own infantry or armoured troops anywhere.

'Support for the infantry in attack is the chief mission of the assault gun by virtue of its armour, manoeuvrability, and cross-country performance and of the rapidity with which it can open fire. The moral support which the infantry receives through its presence is important.

'It does not fire on the move. In close fighting it is vulnerable because its sides are light and it is open-topped. Besides, it has no facilities for

Sturmgeschütz Ausf.B fitted with Kgs 61/400/120 tracks. (Author)

defending itself at close quarters. As it is not in a position to carry out independent reconnaissance and fighting tasks, this weapon must always be supported by infantry.

'In support of an infantry attack, the Sturmgeschütz engages the enemy heavy infantry weapons which cannot be quickly or effectively destroyed by other weapons. In support of a tank attack, it takes over part of the role of the Pz.Kpfw.IV, and deals with enemy anti-tank guns appearing on the front.

'It will only infrequently be employed as divisional artillery, if the tactical and ammunition situation permit. Sturmartillerie is not to be included in the divisional artillery fire plan, but is to be treated only as supplementary, and to be used for special tasks (such as roving batteries). Its employment for its principal tasks must always be assured.

'It is not to be used for anti-tank purposes, and will only engage enemy tanks in self-defence or

where the anti-tank guns cannot successfully deal with them.' (The April 1942 manual states that 'The Sturmgeschütz may be successfully used against armoured vehicles, and light and medium tanks.')

Organisation of the Sturmartillerie-Abteilung and the Sturmbatterie

'The Sturmartillerie-Abteilung consists of headquarters and three batteries. The battery has six guns – three platoons, each of two guns. (The April 1942 manual states that a battery has seven guns, the extra gun being for the battery commander.) The command vehicles for battery and platoon commanders are armoured. Therefore they make it possible for the commanders' to move right up to the foremost infantry line to direct the fire.'

Principles for employment

'The Sturmartillerie-Abteilung are independent units belonging to the High Command. For the conduct of certain engagements, the Abteilung or separate batteries are attached to divisions or to special task forces.

'The division commander should attach some or all of the batteries under his control to infantry or tank units. Only in exceptional circumstances will they be put under the artillery commander.

'Transfer of batteries from support of one unit to another within the division can be carried out very quickly during the course of a battle. Close liaison with the batteries and within the batteries is of primary importance for the timely fulfillment of their missions.

'The Sturmgeschütz fires from positions in open ground, hidden as far as possible from ground and air observation. Only when employed as part of the divisional artillery will these guns fire from covered positions.

'Splitting up of Sturmgeschütz units into small parts (platoons or single guns) jeopardises the fire power and facilitates enemy defence. This should only occur in exceptional cases when the entire Abteilung cannot be employed, such as support of special assault troops or employment over terrain which does not permit observation. If employed singly, mutual fire support and mutual assistance in case of breakdowns and over rough country are

Rear view of a Sturmgeschütz Ausf.B. This vehicle is a later production Ausf.B with the new cast drive sprocket and the armoured housing for the smoke candle rack. (Bundesarchiv 77 3064 4)

not possible.

'As complete a picture as possible must be obtained of the enemy's armour piercing weapons and the positions of his mines. Hasty employment without sufficient reconnaissance might well jeopardise the attack. Premature deployment must also be avoided.

'After an engagement, Sturmgeschütz must not be given security missions, especially at night. They must be withdrawn for refueling, maintenance, and resupply. After four to five days in action, they must be thoroughly serviced. If this is not possible, it must be expected that some will not be fit for action and may fall out. When in rear areas, they must be allotted space near repair shops so that they are readily accessible to maintenance and other facilities.

'Troops cooperating with Sturmgeschütz must give all support possible in dealing with mines and other obstacles. Artillery and heavy infantry

21

of the total ammunition issue), it is possible to lay smoke and to blind enemy weapons which, for example, are sited on the flank. (The April 1942 manual states that the issue is only 10% smoke ammunition).

'Sturmgeschütz render support to tanks usually after the hostile position has been broken into. In this role Sturmbatteries supplement Pz.Kpfw.IVs, and during the fluid stages of the battle direct their fire against enemy anti-tank weapons to the direct front. They follow very closely the first waves of tanks. Destruction of enemy anti-tank weapons on the flanks of an attack will frequently be the task of the Pz.Kpfw.IV.

'Against concrete positions, Sturmgeschütz should be used to engage casemates with armour piercing shells. Cooperation with assault engineers using flamethrowers is very effective in these cases.

'Sturmgeschütz are to be used in towns and woods only in conjunction with particularly strong and close infantry support, but are not to be used if the visibility and field of fire are so limited that firing the guns is impossible without endangering friendly troops. Sturmgeschütz are not suitable for use at night. Their use in snow is also restricted, as they must usually keep to available roads where enemy defence is sure to be met.'

The end of the line for a number of Sturmgeschütz Ausf.B of the Sturmgeschütz-Abteilung 192. These formed part of a large collection of armour captured by the Russians. (Author)

weapons must give support by engaging enemy armour-piercing weapons.

'Surprise is essential for the successful employment of the Sturmartillerie-Abteilung. It is therefore most important for them to move up and into firing positions under cover and generally to commence fire without warning. Stationary batteries fire on targets which are for the moment most dangerous to the infantry (especially enemy heavy infantry weapons), destroy them, and then withdraw to cover in order to avoid enemy fire.

'With the allotment of smoke ammunition (23%

TACTICAL EMPLOYMENT

On the move

'Vehicles on the move should be kept well spaced. Because the average speed of the Sturmgeschütz is about 25 km/h, they must be used in leap-frog fashion when operating with an infantry division. Crossing bridges must be the subject of careful handling. Speed must be reduced to less than 8 km/h and the Sturmgeschütz must keep exactly to the middle of the bridge with intervals of at least 30 m. Bridges must be capable of a load of 20 metric tons. The commander of the Sturmgeschütz must cooperate with the officer in charge of the bridge.'

A Sturmgeschütz Ausf.B at a repair depot after retrofitting the Sfl.ZF1 sight that was originally introduced at the *start of the Sturmgeschütz Ausf.C production run. (Bundesarchiv 274 452 21)*

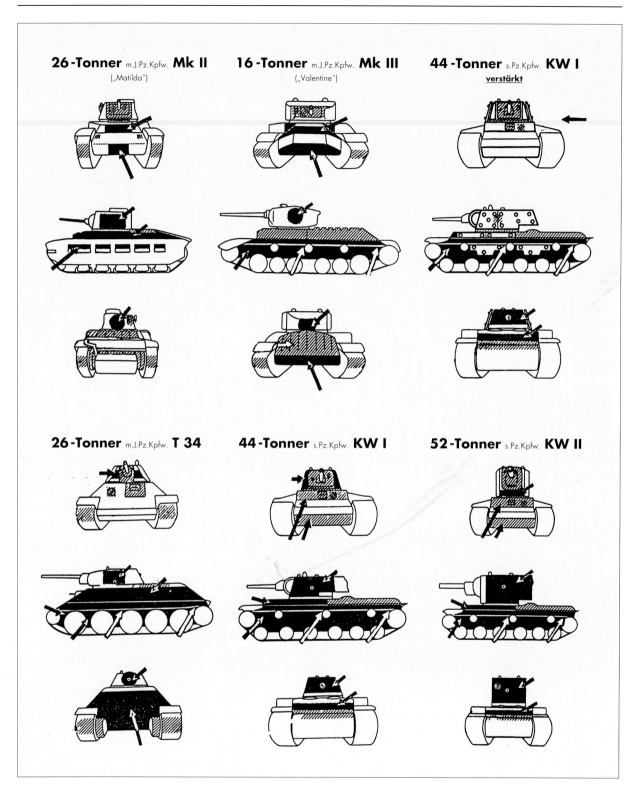

These diagrams identified vulnerable areas on heavily armoured allied tanks. The solid black areas could be penetrated at all ranges by 75mm Gr.38HL/A or HL/A or HL/B (HEAT) shells. The side of the T-34 hull (at ranges up to 100m) and of the Matida hull above the mud chutes (up to 300m) were the only areas vunerable to penetration by 75mm K.Gr. rot Pz. shells from the 75mm Kanone L/24. Hits on stripped areas could cause the tank to be disabled.

1: Versuchsserie 's.Pak' (Experimental series).
Artillerie Lehr Regiment (ALR) in Aterborg 1939

2: Sturmgeschütz. Ausf. A., 16 Sturmbatterie/
Infanterie-Regiment 'GrossDeutschland'

A

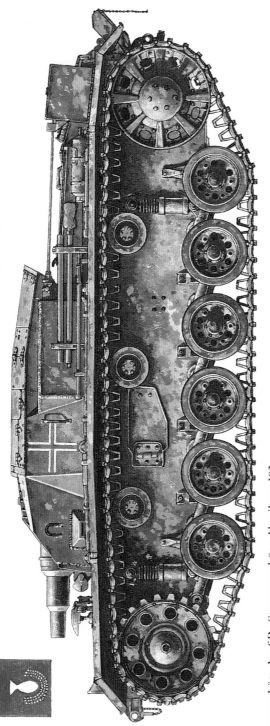

1: Sturmgeschütz Ausf.A., ArtilleriemLehr Regiment, Jüterbog 1941

2: Sturmgeschütz Ausf.B., Sturmgeschütz-Abteilung 192, Russia 1941

B

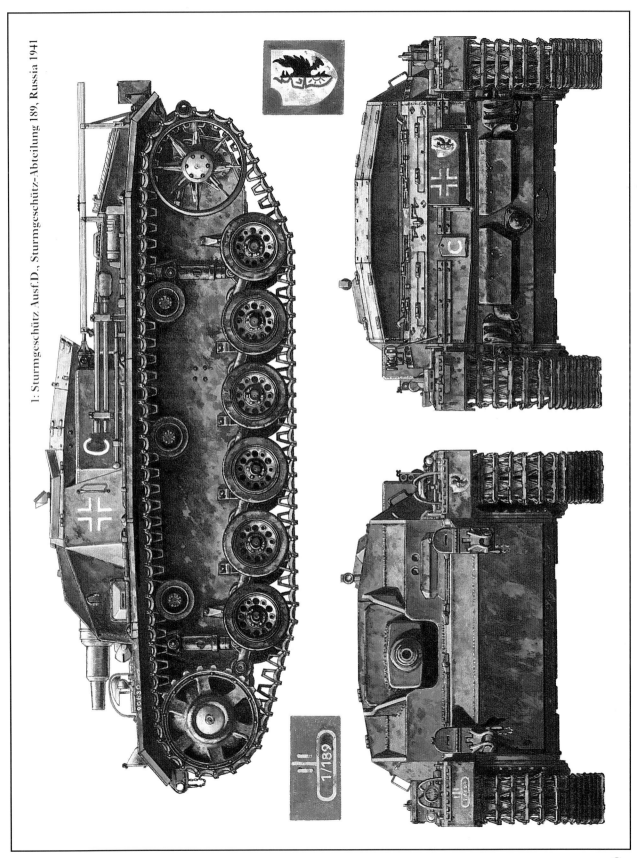

1: Sturmgeschütz Ausf.D., Sturmgeschütz–Abteilung 189, Russia 1941

C

STURMGESCHÜTZ AUSF. B.
Sturmgeschütz-Abteilung 191, Russia 1941

SPECIFICATIONS

Max. speed: 40 km/h

Max. sustained road speed: 25 km/h

Average cross country speed: 10-12 km/h

Radius of action (on roads): 155 km

Radius of action (cross country): 95 km

Trench crossing: 2.3 m

Fording: 0.8 m

Step climbing: 0.6 m

Gradient climbing: 30°

Ground clearance: 0.39 m

Ground pressure: 0.9 kg/cm²

Power-to-weight ratio: 13.5 metric hp/ton

Overall length: 5.40 m

Overall width: 2.92 m

Overall height: 1.95 m

Combat weight (with crew): 20.7 metric tons

Crew: 4 (commander, gunner, loader/ radio operator and driver

KEY

1. Armoured cover for headlight
2. Steering brake inspection hatch
3. Horn
4. Side light
5. 75mm Sturmkanone L/24
6. 50mm frontal armour of superstructure
7. Anti-splash ribbing in front of sight aperture
8. Main ammunition bins on right hand side of gearbox
9. 50mm gun shield
10. 50mm main armour of superstructure
11. Gun carriage
12. Traverse gears
13. Breech of 75mm Sturmkanone L/24
14. Armoured plate to protect gunner's head
15. Gun sight
16. Rubber face protector
17. Recoil guard
18. Collector bag for used shell cases
19. Folding bracket for mounting S.F.14Z periscope
20. Gunner's seat
21. Ammunition for signal pistol
22. Scissors periscope S.F.14Z mounted for use by commander
23. Hand grenades for close-in defence
24. Rear ammunition bin (12 rounds)
25. Loader's hatch
26. S-hook for use with towing cable
27. Commander's voice tube
28. Air duct from air filters to carburettors
29. Fuel filter
30. Right hand side air intake
31. Main fuel tank
32. Jack
33. Carburettors
34. Left hand side motor inspection hatch
35. Jack Maybach V-12 cylinder HL 120 motor
36. Right hand side radiator
37. Spare wheel added by the unit
38. Fan belts and pulley wheel
39. Right hand side inspection hatch
40. Left hand side radiator
41. Smoke grenade launcher (original type)
42. Tow cable holder clips
43. Aerial mount bracket added by unit
44. Left hand side inspection hatch
45. Inertia starter connector cover
46. Warm air outlet under rear armour
47. Folding 2 m rod radio aerial
48. Spare wheel added by the unit
49. Notek distance light
50. Original idler wheel
51. Left side air intake
52. 40mm wide Kgs 61/400/120 continental tyres
53. Fire extinguisher
54. Axe
55. Battery box
56. Wide wheel with 520x95-397 continental tyres
57. Gun cleaning rod set

D

58. Spade	64. Transmission tunnel	71. Driver's seat	78. Cast drive sprocket for
59. Rack for the transmitter of	65. Gunner's seat	72. Gear shift	40mm track
the FuG 16 radio set	66. Gun elevation hand wheel	73. Hydraulic shock absorber	79. Steering brake inspection
60. Crowbar	67. Sight range drum	74. Right hand side steering	and driver escape hatch
61. Suspension bump stop	68. Gun traverse hand wheel	lever	80. 50mm nose armour
62. Suspension swing arm	69. Bridge to carry gun	75. Instrument panel,	
63. Armoured sponson for the	carriage over transmission	(large dial is rev' counter)	
receiver of the FuG 16	tunnel	76. Final drive unit	
radio set	70. SSG 77 gearbox	77. Notek night driving light	

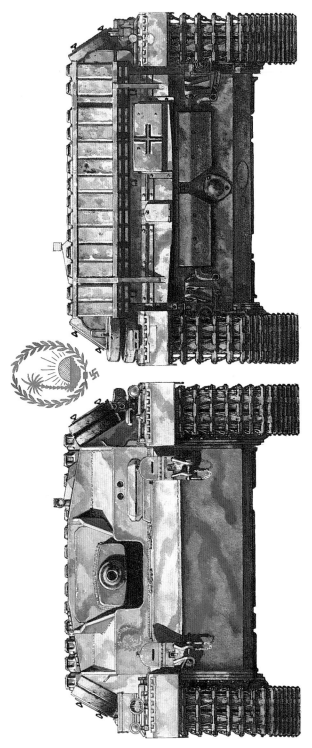

Sturmgeschütz. Ausf.D., Sonder Verband 288, Afrika 1942

E

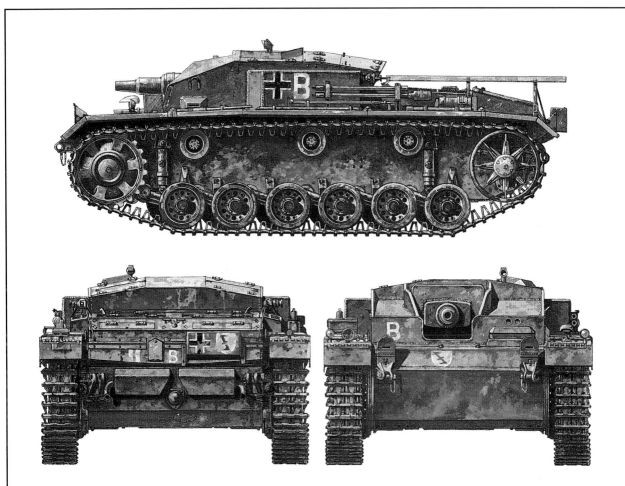

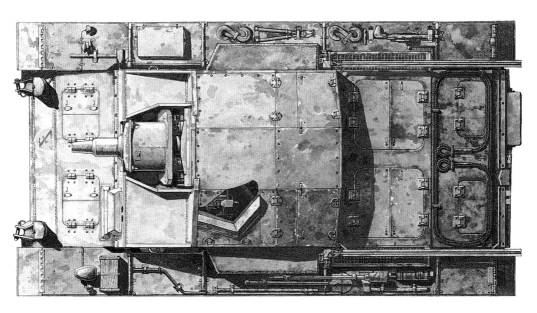

Sturmgeschütz Ausf.E., Sturmgeschütz-Abteilung 249, Russia 1942

Sturmgeschütz Ausf.E., Sturmgeschütz-Abteilung 197, Russia 1942

G

Front view of Sturmgeschütz Ausf.C (Fgst.Nr. 90555) at Jüterborg in February 1942. The new sight projected through the roof and allowed for a redesign of the superstructure's frontal armour. (National Archives)

In the infantry division

'While on the move, the division commander keeps the Sturmartillerie-Abteilung as long as possible under his own control. According to the situation and the terrain, he can, while on the move, place one Sturmbatterie in each combat team. The attachment of these weapons to the advance guard is exceptional. In general, Sturmbatteries are concentrated in the interval between the advance guard and the main body, and are subject to the orders of the column commander. On the march, the battery commander and his party should accompany the column commander.' (The April 1942 manual states that: 'A Sturmgeschütz Batterie well forward in the advance guard may ensure the rapid crushing of enemy resistance.')

In the panzer-division

'On the move, the Sturmartillerie-Abteilung attached to a Panzer-Division can be used to best advantage if included in the advance guard.'

In the attack with an infantry division

'The division commander normally attaches Sturmbatteries to the infantry regiments. On receipt of orders placing him under command of an infantry regiment, the battery commander must report in person to the commander of that infantry regiment. Exhaustive discussion between these two (as to enemy situation, preparation of the regiment for the attack, proposed conduct of the attack, main point of the attack, cooperation with divisional artillery, etc.) will provide the basis for the ultimate employment of the Sturmbatterie.

'It is an error to allot to the battery tasks and targets which can be undertaken by the heavy infantry weapons or the divisional artillery. The Sturmbatterie should rather be employed to engage such nests of resistance as are not known before the beginning of the attack, and which, at the beginning or in the course of the battle cannot be quickly engaged by heavy infantry weapons and artillery. It is the special role of the Sturmbatterie to assist the infantry in fighting its way through deep enemy defence zones. Therefore, it must not be committed until the divisional artillery and the heavy infantry weapons can no longer render adequate support.

'The attached Sturmbatterie can be employed as follows:
1. Before the attack begins, it is located so as to be capable of promptly supporting the regiment's main effort, or
2. The battery is held in the rear, and is only committed if, after the attack begins, a clear picture is obtained of the enemy's dispositions.

'Under both circumstances the attachment of the Sturmbatterie and occasionally of individual platoons, to a battalion may be advantageous.

'The commander under whose command the battery is placed gives the battery commander his orders. The latter makes clear to his platoon com-

Sturmgeschütz Ausf.C entering the Kaserne at Jüterborg in February 1942. (National Archives)

manders the specific battle tasks and shows them, as far as possible on the ground, the targets to be engaged. When in action the battery commander, together with his platoon commanders, must at all times be familiar with the hostile situation and must reconnoitre the ground over which he is to move and attack. The battery will be so disposed by the platoon commanders in the sectors in which it is expected later to operate that, as it approaches the enemy, the battery, under cover, can follow the infantry from sector to sector. How distant an objective can be given, and yet permit the control of fire by the battery and platoon commanders, is dependent on the country, enemy strength, and enemy action. In close country, and when the enemy weapons are well camouflaged, targets cannot be given to the platoons by the battery commander. In these circumstances, fire control falls to the platoon commanders.

'The platoons must then cooperate constantly with the most advanced infantry platoons. They remain close to the infantry and engage the nearest targets. The question of dividing a platoon arises only if individual Sturmgeschütz are allotted to infantry companies or platoons to carry out specific tasks such as for action deep into the enemy's battle position.

'During an attack by tanks supporting an infantry division, the Sturmartillerie-Abteilung engages chiefly anti-tank weapons. In this case too, the Sturmartillerie-Abteilung is attached to infantry elements. Well before the beginning of the tank attack, the batteries are disposed in positions of observation from which they can readily engage enemy anti-tank weapons. They follow up the tanks by platoons and under special conditions, such as in unreconnoitered country, by individual Sturmgeschütz, as soon as possible. In a deep attack, cooperation with tanks leading an infantry attack is possible when the hostile islands of resistance have been disposed of.

'In the enemy tank counter-attack, our own anti-tank guns first engage the hostile tanks. The Sturmartillerie-Abteilung engages the enemy heavy weapons which are supporting the enemy tank counter-attack. Only when the anti-tank guns prove insufficient, do Sturmgeschütz engage enemy tanks. In this case the Sturmgeschütz advance to within effective range of the enemy tanks, halt, and destroy them with anti-tank shells.'

In the attack with a panzer-division

'In such an attack, the following tasks can be carried out by the Sturmartillerie-Abteilung:

1. Support of the tank attack by neutralising enemy anti-tank weapons, and/or
2. Support of the attack by motorised infantry elements.

'According to the situation and the plan of attack, the Abteilung, complete or in part, is attached to the Panzer-Brigade, sometimes with elements attached also to the motorised infantry brigade. Within the Panzer-Brigade, further allotment to Panzer-Regiments is normally necessary. As a rule, complete batteries are attached.

'To support the initial phase of the tank attack, Sturmgeschütz batteries can be placed in positions of observation if suitable ground is already in our possession. Otherwise the batteries follow in the attack close behind the first wave of tanks, and as soon as the enemy is engaged, support the tanks by attacking enemy anti-tank weapons. As the tank attack progresses, it is most important to put enemy defensive weapons out of action as soon as possible. Close support of the leading tanks is the main essential to the carrying out of these tasks.

'The support of the motorised infantry attack is carried out according to the principles for the support of the foot infantry attack.'

In the attack as divisional artillery

'In the attack of a division, the employment of the Sturmartillerie-Abteilung as part of the divisional artillery is exceptional. In this role, the Sturmgeschütz batteries must be kept free for

Sturmgeschütz Ausf.D (Fgst.Nr. 90630) of Sturmgeschütz-Abteilung 189 in Russia. (Bundesarchiv 266 70D32)

Sturmgeschütz Ausf.D (Fgst.Nr. 90869) stationed in Russia. (Bundesarchiv rot 148 160222)

their usual mission at all times and must enter battle with a full issue of ammunition.'

In the pursuit
'In the pursuit, Sturmgeschütz batteries should be close to their own infantry in order to immediately break any enemy resistance. Very close support of the leading infantry units increases their forward momentum. Temporary allotment of individual platoons – under exceptional circumstances, of individual Sturmgeschütz – is possible.'

In the defence
'In the defence, the primary task of Sturmartillerie is the support of counter-thrusts and counter-attacks. The assembly area must be sufficiently far from the friendly battle position to enable the Sturmgeschütz units to move speedily to that sec-

tor which is threatened with a breakthrough. Allotment and employment follow the rules for support of an infantry attack. The point of commitment should be arranged as early as possible with the commanders of the infantry units allocated to the counter-thrust or counter-attack. In the defence as in the attack, the Sturmartillerie-Abteilung will only be employed in an anti-tank role if it must defend itself against a tank attack (only 12% of the ammunition issue is armour piercing). (In the April 1942 manual, 15% of the ammunition was AP). If employed as part of the divisional artillery (which is rare), the Abteilung will be placed under the division artillery commander.'

In the withdrawal
'For the support of infantry in withdrawal, batteries, and even individual platoons or Sturmgeschütz, are allotted to infantry units. By virtue of their armour, Sturmgeschütz are able to

engage enemy targets even when the infantry has already withdrawn. To assist disengagement from the enemy, tank attacks carried out with limited objectives can be supported by Sturmgeschütz. Allotment of Sturmgeschütz batteries or platoons to rear parties or rear guards is effective.'

ORGANISATION

The SS-Sturmgeschütz-Batterie of LSSAH received the last six Ausf.A of the 1. Serie. (Author)

The first unit, Sturmbatterie 640, was already raised on 1 November 1939 before the first production series Sturmgeschütz left the factory. The next two units, Sturmbatterie 659 and 660, were created on 8 April 1940 and the fourth unit, Sturmbatterie 665 was created on 9 May 1940. On 10 April 1940, Sturmbatterie 640 became an organic part of Infanterie-Regiment 'Grossdeutschland' and was renamed as the 16.Sturmbatterie. These four batteries were the only units with Sturmgeschütz created in time to take part in the offensive through Belgium and France in May and June 1940.

The official organisation of the Sturmbatterie

was specified in K.St.N.445 dated 1 November 1939. The battery of six vehicles was divided into three platoons each in possession of two Sturmgeschütz (Sd.Kfz.142). In addition each independent Sturmbatterie was to have five leichte gepanzerten Beobachtungswagen (Sd.Kfz.253) (Light Armoured Observation Vehicle) for the platoon leaders and battery commanders, six leichte gepanzerte Munitionstransportkraftwagen (Sd.Kfz.252) (Light Armoured Ammunition

Sturmgeschütz Ausf.D (Fgst.Nr. 90683) was one of three Sturmgeschütz which served in North Africa with Sonder Verband 288. This was a tropicalised vehicle with additional air intakes cut into the rear deck access hatches that were covered by armour cowls. (Tank Museum)

Carrier) towing gepanzerte Anhänger (1 Achs) (Sd.Anh.32/1), and three mittlere Mannschafttransportwagen (Sd.Kfz.251) (Medium Armoured Troop Carrier) for replacement crews. Due to delays in production of these armoured support vehicles, other armoured vehicles were substituted including Panzerkampfwagen I (Sd.Kfz.101), kleine Panzerbefehlswagen (Sd.Kfz.265) (Command Vehicle), and Panzerkampfwagen I (A) Munitions-Schlepper (Sd.Kfz.111) (Ammunition Tractor).

The last six Sturmgeschütz Ausf.A from the first series were originally intended for the Fifth Independent Battery (Sturmbatterie 666 created on 20 May 1940). Instead they were given to an SS Sturmbatterie created on 20 May 1940 for the Leibstandarte 'Adolf Hitler'. Sturmbatterie 666 and Sturmbatterie 667 (created on 1 July 1940) were issued the Sturmgeschütz Ausf.A based on the modified Pz.Kpfw.III Ausf.G chassis.

After the war, the story emerged that Sturmbatterie 666 and 667 were not sent into France because their Sturmgeschütz could not be used in combat. The excuse was that bolts holding the additional armour on the hull front were cylindrical in shape and therefore would be propelled into the fighting compartment when hit. The simple truth is that these two batteries were issued Sturmgeschütz too late to participate in the campaign in the West. The practice of bolting on additional armour with cylindrical bolts did not present a significant hazard, was quite common on several models of the Pz.Kpfw.III, Pz.Kpfw.IV and Sturmgeschütz, and continued to the end of the war with every Sturmgeschütz Ausf.G.

Starting on 10 August 1940, the Sturmartillerie was organised into Abteilungen each with three batteries of six Sturmgeschütz. The official table of organisation for the batteries belonging to an Abteilung was K.St.N.446 dated 7 July 1940. Retaining the same number of Sturmgeschütz as the independent batteries, the number of armoured support vehicles was decreased to three Sd.Kfz.253 and three Sd.Kfz.252.

General Order Number 99 dated 7 February 1941, officially changed the name from Sturmartillerie-Abteilung to Sturmgeschütz-Abteilung and the name of the independent batteries was changed to Sturmgeschütz-Batterie.

Between 10 August 1940 and 10 January 1942, 18 Sturmartillerie Abteilungen were formed and issued Sturmgeschütz with the 75 mm Kanone L/24 before production shifted to the longer 75 mm Sturmkanone 40 L/43 in March 1942. In addition an independent unit, Sturmgeschütz-Lehr-Batterie 900, was formed, as well as three batteries that were assigned as an organic part to SS Divisions 'Das Reich', 'Totenkopf' and 'Wiking'. By 1 March 1941, newly created Sturmgeschütz-Batteries were authorised by special orders to possess a seventh Sturmgeschütz for the battery commander and to mount transmitting radio sets into one of the two Sturmgeschütz in each platoon for the platoon commander. The specific orders dated 1 April 1941 for creating Sturmgeschütz-Batterie 900, authorised the following changes to K.St.N.445, Batterie 75 mm Sturmgeschütz (6 Geschütz)(mot S) dated 1.2.41:

'In the place of five leichte gepanzerte Beobachtungskraftwagen (Sd.Kfz.253), one Sturmgeschütz (as command and observation vehicle for the battery commander) and four heavy motorcycles with sidecars for dismounted platoon leaders; in the place of three Zugkraftwagen (3t) (Sd.Kfz.11), three medium trucks; and in the place of one Zugkraftwagen (1t) (Sd.Kfz.10), one light truck.'

By a general order dated 7 May 1941, every independent Sturmgeschütz-Batterie with K.St.N.445 dated 1 February 1941 and every Sturmgeschütz-Batterie in an Abteilung with K.St.N.446 dated 1 February 1941 were to be reorganised under K.St.N.446 dated 18 April 1941. This new organisation authorised every previously created Sturmgeschütz-Batterie to possess a seventh Sturmgeschütz for the battery commander. Thus all Sturmgeschütz-Batteries were authorised to possess seven Sturmgeschütz before the attack on Russia (Operation 'Barbarossa') kicked off on 22 June 1941. However, a few of these batteries had yet to be issued their seventh Sturmgeschütz by this date.

Combat and experience reports

In presenting an overview of how the Sturmgeschütz fared in combat, only original

combat and experience reports are used to relate the thoughts of the troops that fought in the Sturmgeschütz. This establishes a foundation for the reader to evaluate its performance free from the influence of assumptions, generalities, opinions, and other uninformed statements expressed by armchair armour experts. The reader should be aware that these original experience reports are biased and do not describe the 'routine'. Most of the German reports were written with the motive of initiating improvements to the Sturmgeschütz or changing tactics.

First Sturmgeschütz in action

The first Sturmgeschütz action in May 1940 involved the 16.Sturmbatterie, assigned as an organic part of the 'Grossdeutschland' Infanterie-Regiment. 'Grossdeutschland' operated in the breakthrough at Sedan under General Guderian's Korps. A motorised platoon, with two anti-tank guns attached, constituted the leading element of our advance guard as we marched west from Vance (20 miles west of Luxembourg) to Etalle. As these vehicles approached Etalle, they encountered hostile armoured cars. During the ensuing engagement, a report was received at regimental

This front three-quarter view of Sturmgeschütz Ausf.D (Fgst.Nr. 90683) shows the driver's visor knocked off by a shell hit. The racks and spare roadwheel mounts were added by the unit. The circular straps over the side intakes are mounts for special pre-cleaning air filters, which gave additional protection to the engine in dusty conditions. (Tank Museum)

headquarters that Villers was occupied by French cavalry. The II.Bataillon was ordered to attack Villers immediately. After a three-hour advance against increasing resistance this battalion arrived at the eastern edge of the village, where further progress was checked by strong hostile fire.

'In the meanwhile, the I.Bataillon, with the Sturmbatterie attached, had arrived at Neuhabich, where the battalion commander ordered a rifle company to gain contact with the II.Bataillon. Advancing slowly south from Neuhabich, the rifle company finally reached Villers where it, likewise, met heavy resistance. Then, the company commander sent the following oral message to the rear: 'Sturmbatterie to the front!'

'The third platoon of the Sturmbatterie dashed forward to engage in its first fight. The platoon commander, Lt. Franz, wearing a steel helmet, stood erect in the turret of his command vehicle.

A Sturmgeschütz Ausf.E (Fgst.Nr. 90773) with the super-structure of an Ausf.D – an arrangement which typifies the gradual changes introduced to the vehicle during its production run.

He was followed by Sturmgeschütz Nr.5 and Nr.6. 'The platoon encountered no resistance until arriving at the centre of town where it received heavy machine-gun fire. The platoon leader answered this fire with his MP (sub-machine gun). Two rounds from each of the Sturmgeschütz silenced the machine guns.

'Then Sturmgeschütz Nr.6 went into action, firing at the nearby buildings. One shell exploded in a courtyard among some French cavalry horses. The uninjured animals galloped away, crazed with fright. Sturmgeschütz Nr.5 swung into position in the church yard. Hostile machine guns were firing from two windows in a large building close by.

The platoon commander ordered the gun commander to fire on this target. These machine guns were silenced by one round from the Sturmgeschütz. Finally, the enemy evacuated the main street and the centre of the town, but machine gun resistance was renewed at the western edge of the village. Momentarily, it was thought that the Sturmgeschütz should be sent ahead again. But the riflemen and anti-tank weapons (Panzerjäger partially armoured on self-propelled mounts), were able to reduce this resistance unassisted. The II.Bataillon remained in the town during the night. Field kitchens were moved up, the men were fed, and medical personnel cared for the wounded. 'The third platoon of the Sturmbatterie obtained some rest just in rear of the front line, the men sleeping in their vehicles. The advance guard, with the third platoon of the

Sturmbatterie attached, moved out at 0500 the next morning. The Sturmgeschütz advanced to the destroyed bridge across a tributary of the Semois river. The pioneers, although hard at work, had not yet completed their task here, so the guns forded the river. The regimental commander, in order to get up to the front, took a seat in an Sturmbatterie ammunition vehicle.

'After fording the stream, the Sturmgeschütz came to a barricade composed of tree trunks, which obstructed the road leading up a slope in one of the southern spurs of the Ardennes forest. The driver of Sturmgeschütz Nr.5 stepped on his accelerator, dashed against the obstacle and opened the way. So far, no enemy had been encountered. The infantry was in the lead as the advance guard moved through Mellier into a beechwood forest beyond that town. Resistance was encountered at 1030 while moving through a clearing in the woods. The I.Bataillon, upon emerging from the forests, was fired upon from the direction of Suxy. The leading company deployed promptly and, supported by an anti-tank (Pak) platoon, began to advance toward the town.

The regimental and battalion commanders, accompanied by certain members of their staffs, observed the action from high ground east of Suxy. The advance of this battalion was checked at the stream just west of the town. Activity prevailed at the command posts. Heavy weapons were ordered up. Tasks were assigned and positions designated. As the heavy infantry weapons and Sturmgeschütz were heard approaching from the rear, the battalion commander, in a quick decision, signalled his advance reserve company to turn off and attack in the new direction.

'Within five minutes of their arrival, the heavy weapons opened fire. In the meantime, the Sturmbatterie continued to the front to assist the leading rifle companies. The riflemen slowly worked their way ahead, pressing hard against the enemy, driving him off of the high ground to the right front. Finally one of the Sturmgeschütz moved up onto this commanding terrain and quickly fired eleven rounds at a range of 800 m into a battery of enemy horse artillery going into

The Sturmgeschütz Ausf.E is identified by the extended panniers on both sides of the superstructure, which were used to house additional radio equipment. (Bundesarchiv rot 69/89/7)

action. Then, this Sturmgeschütz itself was taken under fire by a French anti-tank battery.

'In the meantime, the German artillery opened fire and the battalion began to advance across the Vierre River. As usual, all the bridges had been destroyed. Hence, all trucks had to be left behind, but the water was no obstacle for the infantry and the Sturmartillerie.

'After crossing the river, the advance was checked again by resistance coming principally from a fortified house, standing along the route of advance. Sturmgeschütz Nr.5 went into action against this house. The first round hit the lower left window; the second entered the attic window; the third went over the house but exploded among some retreating Frenchmen. By 1730, all resistance in this vicinity had been overcome.

'The French reconnaissance battalion, which had attempted to stop the regiment, was completely destroyed. The advance continued, but the next 15 km could only be covered by foot, because the trucks could not be moved across the river. But the day's objective was reached at 2100 and even exceeded during the night.

'The performance of the Sturmbatterie, in its initial engagements at Villers and Suxy, completely won the hearts of the infantrymen. These weapons gave valuable and timely assistance to the foot soldier in battle. They also assisted the infantry on the march by carrying light MGs and mortars, and towing ammunition carts. The next morning the regiment moved through St. Medard and Herbeumont. On the following day (13 May), the regiment left Belgian soil, marching through Bouillon into the Boise de Sedan, and on the next morning (14 May) it forced a crossing over the Meuse at Sedan, thereby clearing the road to the north for the oncoming Panzer Divisions.'

EARLY SUCCESS IN RUSSIA

During the first '15 weeks' of the campaign in the East, Oberleutnant Pelikan's Sturmgeschütz-Batterie shot up 91 tanks, captured 23 tanks, knocked out 23 bunkers, and destroyed ten trains and hundreds of trucks loaded with supplies. Pelikan's first encounter with Red Army tanks occurred around Bialystock: 'Four Sturmgeschütz formed the point for a bicycle company advanced guard. Four enemy tanks appeared and charged toward the Germans. The Sturmgeschütz halted. The crews went to work as calm and collected as in the barracks yard. The tanks had advanced to within 20 m when all four Sturmgeschütz opened fire. A short, hard firefight ensued. Two tanks remained stationary. The other two, hit and burning, continued moving. Running around confused, they rushed past the Sturmgeschütz and stopped after a few hundred metres. Four tank kills already in the first fight.

'The advance rolled forward through a village in a depression, then up onto the plain. Now it became clear that the four tanks were an advance patrol. The mass of the Soviet forces wanted to try to stop our advance here. They were already closing on our advance guard. Tanks of all sizes in increasing numbers advanced at high speed from all sides. The bicycle company took cover in a square formation. The Sturmgeschütz took up defensive positions, one facing each point on the compass.

'Like hornets the tanks swarmed around the small area occupied by the defenders. They charged, quickly braked, and opened fire, while their tracks threw up thick clouds of dust. The Sturmgeschütz fired at whatever appeared. Knocked out tanks lay in rows, but the Bolsheviks continued to send in more tanks.

'The unit was completely surrounded. Soon the heat was unbearable. The dust attacked the eyes and throat. At great personal sacrifice, the bicyclist brought water. Appreciatively, the crews cooled their faces and hands. Again and again, new tanks appeared out of the dust clouds and smoke from burning tanks. Often they were first visible at only ten metres in front of the guns.

'Finally, after two hours of continuous fire fight, a short pause ensued. Apparently the Bolsheviks needed to pause to take a breath. Looking over the battlefield, 32 tanks remained stationary. Then a second Sturmgeschütz-Batterie and a Flak-Batterie came up in relief.

'Still the Soviets attacked many more times

The rear of a Sturmgeschütz Ausf.E; note the twin radio antenna. (Bundesarchiv rot 76/70/33)

before being forced to retreat. Drawing a deep breath, the Sturmgeschütz commanders determined the remaining ammunition supply. Each Sturmgeschütz only had four rounds left. The Soviet tank force assault had been broken by our Sturmgeschütz.'

Experience on the roads to Leningrad

The commander of Sturmgeschütz-Abteilung 185 wrote a detailed experience report covering the period from 22 June/31 December 1941. The following excerpts from this report refute many conventional views on the capabilities and tactics employed by the Sturmgeschütz with the shorter 75 mm Kanone L/24.

'Having not had time to reorganise under the latest K.St.N., at the start of the campaign each battery consisted of 161 men, six Sturmgeschütz, three armoured command vehicles (Sd.Kfz.253), six ammunition half-tracks (three Sd.Kfz.252 and three Sd.Kfz.10), three 3-ton half-tracks for replacement crews, one 1-ton signals half-track, eight cars, 14 trucks, and thirteen motorcycles of which two had sidecars.

'Two of the batteries were organised as three platoons each with two Sturmgeschütz, the third battery as two platoons each with three Sturmgeschütz. Both organisations proved equally effective during the early part of the campaign. But as the campaign dragged on, the Sturmgeschütz required frequent repairs and breakdowns occured daily, the organisation with two platoons proved to be more useful. As a result, in the last part of the campaign this organisation was ordered for the entire Abteilung, as in most cases only one Sturmgeschütz was operational per platoon. The two platoon organisation

Sturmgeschütz Ausf.E of Sturmgeschütz-Abteilung 192 overpainted in whitewash for the Russian winter. (Author)

had a secondary advantage in that an armoured command vehicle (Sd.Kfz.253) became available for the battery commander. There was no future in driving an open car through enemy gunfire.

'The crew of the Sturmgeschütz had two advantages over infantry: 1) a better and unhindered view of the terrain (the Sturmgeschütz is a mobile observation tower in comparison to the infantry under cover) and 2) high-power optical instruments. Because of this, it was seldom the case that infantry identified targets first and showed them to the Sturmgeschütz. Without waiting for special directions or support from other weapons, the Sturmgeschütz was alone responsible for seeking out and destroying targets. It was disadvantageous to burden the Sturmgeschütz with specific tactical directions, because they are restricted enough in their employment by terrain obstacles (such as woods, marsh, water, trenches, mines, etc.). Already by the third day, the enemy had employed tanks. However, the Sturmgeschütz always proved to be superior until the 52-ton tanks (KW-I) appeared at Leningrad. It was especially difficult to recognise enemy mine barriers in the snow. One Sturmgeschütz was totally destroyed when it ran onto a new type of mine.

The commander and loader both were killed when thrown 12 metres from the Sturmgeschütz. No help could be provided to the other crew members still inside the burning Sturmgeschütz. Due to the harsh winter and worn out Sturmgeschütz, many further breakdowns occurred, including damaged transmissions, failure of all the starters, broken torsion bars, and broken and sprung tracks. On 10 December the Abteilung was left with only five conditionally operational Sturmgeschütz. Three further Sturmgeschütz were blown up to prevent capture after breaking down where they could not be recovered due to enemy action. By 17 December, the Abteilung was down to one operational Sturmgeschütz.

'From 22 June/31 December 1941, in exchange for the total loss of nine Sturmgeschütz (six destroyed by enemy action and three blown up to prevent capture), Sturmgeschütz-Abteilung 185 destroyed or captured 64 medium and heavy artillery pieces, 66 light artillery pieces, 39 infantry guns, 34 mortars, 79 anti-tank guns, 45 anti-aircraft guns, 314 MGs, 91 tanks, nine armoured cars, etc. No less than 58,890 rounds of 75 mm ammunition had been fired. The high rate of ammunition expenditure was due to the order from the commander of the 18th Army that Sturmgeschütz were to use gunfire to open routes for the infantry to advance.'

In a follow-up report for the period from 20 February/9 April 1942, Sturmgeschütz-Abteilung 185 claimed to have knocked out two KW-II, 29 KW-I, and 27 T-34 tanks and over 50 guns against a total loss of eight Sturmgeschütz. Only those enemy tanks that were observed to be burning or heavily damaged were claimed. No claims were made for those stopped by damaging the tracks, drive sprocket, etc. Personnel losses had amounted to 11 dead and 23 wounded. The ammunition expenditure during this period was 12,370 Sprenggranaten (HE shells), 5,120 K.Gr.rot Pz. (AP shells), and 1,360 Gr.38 HL (HEAT) rounds.

THE PLATES

Plate A1: *Versuchsserie 's. Pak' (Experimental series). Artillerie Lehr Regiment (ALR) in Äterbog 1939*

This experimental series of five 's. Pak' was delivered by Daimler-Benz. The chassis was from the Pz.Kpfw.III Ausf.B. The superstructures were built from soft steel and initially were open topped. The roof was added in 1939. The experimental 75 mm Sturmkanone L/24 guns were delivered by Krupp. Armoured vehicles of this period were painted in a camouflage of irregular patterns of dunkelgrau RAL 7021 (Dark grey) and dunkelbraun RAL 7017 (Dark brown). These 's. Pak' Versuchsserie vehicles were used as training vehicles by the Artillerie Lehr Regiment (ALR) in Jüterbog at least until the end of 1941. The emblem of the ALR was reproduced on the left front and right rear mudflaps and on the superstructure front plate alongside the driver visor. The five vehicles had an identifying letter A through to E on the left of the superstructure front plate.

Plate A2: *Sturmgeschütz Ausf.A (Fgst.Nr. 90001 -90030) 16. Sturmbatterie/Infanterie-Regiment 'Grossdeutschland'*

The first unit of Sturmgeschütz, Sturmbatterie 640, was founded in November 1939 before

This Sturmgeschutz was assembled from a mixture of components. The superstructure is from an Ausf.B., while the hull appears to be that of an Ausf.F. with additional 30mm plates welded to the front armour. (Tank Museum)

the first Sturmgeschütz Ausf.A were delivered by Daimler-Benz. On 10 April 1940 the Sturmbatterie 640 became part of Infanterie-Regiment 'Grossdeutschland' and was renamed 16. Sturmbatterie. During the invasion of France, Sturmgeschütz of 'Grossdeutschland' were the first Sturmgeschütz to see action. German armour of this period was painted in dunkelgrau RAL 7021 (Dark grey) and dunkelbraun RAL 7017 (Dark brown). Sturmgeschütz of 'Grossdeutschland' were marked with the national insignia, a 'Balkankreuz' in black and white and the vehicle tactical number in white. From October 1939 other vehicles of 'Grossdeutschland' were marked with the white steel helmet emblem surrounded by a square, circle, triangle and diamond depending on whether they were assigned to the I., II., III. or IV. Bataillon. 16. Sturmbatterie was part of IV. Bataillon, but insufficient photographs exist to show whether such a marking was carried.

Plate B1: *Sturmgeschütz Ausf. A (Fgst. Nr. 90401-90420) Artillerie Lehr Regiment (ALR) in Jüterbog in 1941*
In June and July 1940 a series of 20 Sturmgeschütz was built using the chassis of Pz. Kpfw.III Ausf.G. These were initially issued to Sturmbatterie 666 and 667 but too late for them to be involved in the invasion of France. Some of these Ausf. A were used as training vehicles by the ALR in Jüterbog. From June 1940, newly produced German armoured vehicles were painted only in dunkelgrau RAL 7021 (Dark grey).

Plate B2: *Sturmgeschütz Ausf. B, Sturmgeschütz-Abteilung 192, Russia 1941.*
The Sturmgeschütz-Abteilung 192 was founded on 25 November 1940. In April 1942 the Sturmgeschütz-Abteilung 192 was renamed Sturmgeschütz-Abteilung "Grossdeutschland" The Sturmgeschütz Ausf.B of the Sturmgeschütz-Abteilung 192 were painted in dunkelgrau RAL 7021 (Dark grey). The front and rear mudflaps had their outer edges outlined in white. Markings include the Sturmgeschütz-Abteilung 192 'Totenkopf' emblem (Death's head) in yellow on a black rectangle (Some vehicles had this in white

painted directly on to the base camouflage colour) on the front right and either side of the superstructure and the rear armour of the smoke candle rack. The 'Balkankreuz' was in black was a white outline on either side of the superstructure. Each Sturmgeschütz carried an identifying serif style number, on each side of the superstructure, on the front right of the superstructure and on the tail plate.

Plate C: *Sturmgeschütz Ausf. D, Fgst.Nr. 90630, Sturmgeschütz-Abteilung 189, Russia 1941*
On 9 July 1941 the Sturmgeschütz-Abteilung 189 was founded. Four weeks were allowed for the unit to be ready for action. In August 1941 Sturmgeschütz-Abteilung 189 was shipped by rail to Russia. They were engaged in heavy fighting for the rest of the year in the area of Witebsk and later Wjasma. This Sturmgeschütz Ausf.D was completed by Alkett in June 1941. As with all German armoured vehicles of this period, it was painted in dunkelgrau RAL 7021 (Dark grey). Marking include the Sturmgeschütz-Abteilung 189 'Ritter/Adler' emblem (knight and eagle crests combined) on the front left mudflap and the rear armour of the smoke candle rack. The 'Balkankreuz' was a white painted outline. Each Sturmgeschütz carried an identifying letter on the superstructur and on the tail plate. The Sturmgeschütz company organisational symbol was carried on the front right hand side mud flap.

Plate D: *Sturmgeschütz Ausf.B, Sturmgeschütz-Abteilung 191, Russia 1941*
The cutaway drawing shows a Sturmgeschütz Ausf.B issued to Sturmgeschütz-Abteilung 191 in October 1940. The exterior was painted in the dunkelgrau RAL 7021 (Dark grey). The markings were the outline 'Balkankreuz' in white on either side of the superstructure. The Büffel (Bison) emblem of the Sturmgeschütz-Abteilung 191 was also painted on either side of the superstructure, on the right front mud flap, and to the left of the starter cover on the rear plate of the motor compartment. The emblem itself was a red Bison painted in a black rectangle outlined in red. The tactical

identification letter, in this case a white 'C' was painted on the starter cover itself. The Sturmgeschütz company organisational symbol painted in yellow was carried on the front left mud flap. The fighting compartment interior was painted in elfenbein RAL 1002 (Ivory). Radio sets were dunkelgrau RAL 7021 (Dark grey). The engine compartment was left in rot RAL 8012 (Red primer).

Plate E: *Sturmgeschütz Ausf.D. Sonder Verband 288 Afrika 1942*

Although only three Sturmgeschütz Ausf.D were sent to North Africa, these are well known as this particular vehicle (Fgst.Nr. 90683) was extensively examined and photographed after its capture by the British forces. Built by Alkett in July 1941, it was collected by the crew on 20 August 1941 and transported to Greece. In early 1942 the unit was shipped to Africa. It was in action at Bir Hacheim in May, Acroma in June and El Alamein in October 1942. This Sturmgeschütz was modified for 'tropical' use by cutting openings in five of the six hatches on the rear engine deck. These openings, covered by armoured cowls, increased the flow of air through the engine compartment. A set of cylindrical containers housing air filters for pre-cleaning air to the carburettors were mounted on both sides above the main cooling air intakes. The unit added additional racks for carrying fuel and water cans. For use in tropical areas these Sturmgeschütz were repainted according to the March 1941 order which specified that armoured vehicles be painted in gelbbraun RAL 8000 (Olive brown) and graubraun RAL 7008 (Khaki grey). The 'Balkankreuz' was painted on with an outline of black in turn outlined in white. This was repeated on the sides and on the smoke candle rack at the rear. The crest of the Sonderverband 288, a green laurel wreath surrounding a palm tree and rising sun over a small swastika, was painted on the right front superstructure plate.

Plate F: *Sturmgeschütz Ausf.E, Sturmgeschütz-Abteilung 249, Russia 1942*

The Sturmgeschütz-Abteilung 249, founded on the 10 January 1942 was the last of Sturmgeschütz-Abteilung which was initially equipped with Sturmgeschütz armed with the 75 mm Kanone L/24. The Ausf.E had been in production since September 1941 and was replaced by the Ausf.F in March 1942. The Ausf.E can be identified by the longer sponsons on both sides of the superstructure. The Sturmgeschütz Ausf.E of the Sturmgeschütz-Abteilung 249 were painted in dunkelgrau RAL 7021 (Dark grey). Markings include the Sturmgeschütz-Abteilung 249 'Wolfangel' emblem (A black flash on a yellow shield outlined in white) on the front upper nose armour plate and the rear armour of the smoke candle rack. The 'Balkankreuz' was painted in black with a white outline on either side of the superstructure and on the rear armour of the smoke candle rack. Each Sturmgeschütz carried an identifying letter on each side of the superstructure, on the front right of the superstructure and on the tail plate.

Plate G: *Sturmgeschütz Ausf.E, Sturmgeschütz-Abteilung 197, Russia 1942*

The Sturmgeschütz-Abteilung 197, founded on the 25 November 1940 and served in Southern Russia. As with all German armoured vehicles of this period, it was painted in dunkelgrau RAL 7021 (Dark grey). Marking include the Sturmgeschütz-Abteilung 197 'Kanoner Adler' emblem (A black eagle clutching grenades on a white shield) on the front right of the upper nose armour plate and the rear armour of the smoke candle dispenser. The 'Balkankreuz' was painted in black with a white outline. Each Sturmgeschütz of Sturmgeschütz-Abteilung 197 carried an identifying letter, normally A, B, C etc. on both side of the superstructure and on rear plate. In this case the letter was replaced by 'Z1'.

Notes sur les planches en couleur

A1 'S. Pak' Versuchsserie (Série expérimentale). Artillerie Lehr Regiment (ALR) a Aterborg 1939. Cette série expérimentale de cinq 'S. Pak' fut livrée par Daimler-Benz. Le châssis venait du Pz. Kptw. III Aust. B. Les superstructures étaient en acier tendre et étaient initialement sans toit. Le toit fut ajouté

Farbtafeln

A1 "s.Pak"-Versuchsserie. Artillerie-Lehrregiment (ALR) in Jüterbog 1939 Diese Versuchsserie von fünf "s.Pak" wurde von Daimler-Benz geliefert. Das Fahrgestell stammte vom Pz. Kpfw.III Ausf.B. Die Aufbauten bestanden aus Weichstahl und hatten usprünglich kein Dach, das aber dann 1939 hinzugefügt

en 1939. Les canons expérimentaux 7.5 cm Stumkanone L/24 furent livrés par Krupp. Les véhicules blindés de cette époque étaient peints selon un camouflage de motifs irréguliers en dunkelgrau RAL 7021 (gris foncé) et dunkelbraun RAL 7017 (marron foncé). Ces cinq véhicules portaient une lettre d'identification de A à E sur la gauche de la plaque avant de la superstructure. **A2** Sturmgeschatz Aust A (Fgst Nr. 90001-90030) 16. Sturmbatterie/Infanterie-Regiment 'Grossdeutschland' La première unité de la Sturmgeschatz, Sturmbatterie 540, fut fondée en novembre 1939 avant la livraison du premier Sturmgeschatz Aust A par Daimler-Benz.

B1 Sturmgeschatz Aust. A (Fgst. Nr. 90401 - 90420) Artillerie Lehr Regiment (ALR) à Jaterbog en 1941 En juin et juillet 1940, une série de 20 Sturmgeschatz fut construite avec le châssis du Pz. Kpfw. III Aust. G. Initialement, ils furent attribués à la Sturmbatterie 666 et 667 mais trop tard pour qu'ils puissent participer à l'invasion de la France. Certains de ces nouveaux Aust A furent utilisés comme véhicules de formation par l'ALR à Jaterbog. A partir de juin 1940, le blindage allemand fut peint uniquement en dunkelgrau RAL 7021 (gris foncé). **B2** Sturmgeschatz Ausf. B, Sturmgeschatz-Abteilung 192, Russia 1941 Le Sturmgeschatz-Abteilung 192 fut fondé le 25 novembre 1940. En avril 1942, le Sturmgeschatz-Abteilung 192 fut rebaptisé Sturmgeschatz-Abteilung 'Grossdeutschland'. Les Sturmgeschatz Ausf. B du Sturmgeschatz-Abteilung 192 étaient peints en dunkelgrau RAl 7021 (gris foncé).

C Sturmgeschatz Aust. D, Fgst Nr. 90630, Sturmgeschatz-Abteilung 189, Russia 1941 Le 9 juillet 1941, le Sturmgeschatz-Abteilung 189 fut créé. On donna quatre semaines à cette unité pour se préparer au combat. Ce Sturmgeschatz Ausf D fut terminé par Alkett en juin 1941. Comme c'est le cas de tous les véhicules allemands blindés de cette époque, il fut peint en dunkelgrau RAL 7021 (gris foncé). Parmi les marquages, citons l'emblème 'Ritte/rAdler' (couronne de chevalier et d'aigle combinées) Sturmgeschatz-Abteilung 189 sur le garde-boue avant gauche et sur le blindage du diffuseur de fumée. Le 'Balkankreuz' était une bordure blanche peinte.

D Sturmgeschatz Aust. B, Sturmgeschatz-Abteilung 191, Russia 1941 Cet écorché représenten un Sturmgeschatz Aust. B émis au Sturmgeschatz-Abteiling 191 qui avait été créé en octobre 1940. L'extérieur était peint en dunkelgrau RAL 7021 (gris foncé). Les marques étaient la silhouette 'Balkankreuz' blanche de chaque côté de la superstructure. L'emblème Baffel (Buffle) du Sturmgeschatz-Abteilung 191 était également peint des deux côtés de la superstructure, sur le garde-boue avant droit et sur le gauche du couvercle du starter sur la plaque arrière du logement du moteur. L'emblème lui-même était un buffle rouge peint dans un rectangle noir bordé de rouge.

E Ssturmgeschatz Aust. D. Sonder Verband 288 Afrika 1942 Bien que seulement trois Sturmbeschatz Aust. D furent envoyés en Afrique du Nord, ils sont tous bien connus car ce véhicule particulier (Fgst. Nr 90683) fut beaucoup examiné et photographié après sa capture par les forces britanniques. Début 1942, cette unité fut expédiée en Afrique. Elle participa aux combats de Bir Hacheim en mai, Acroma en juin et El Alamein en octobre 1942. Dans les régions tropicales, ces Sturmgeschatz étaient repeints selon l'ordre de mars 1941 qui spécifiait que les véhicules blindés devaient être peints en gelbbraun RAl 8000 (marron olive) et graubraun RAL 7008 (gris kaki).

F Sturmgeschatz Aust. E, Sturmgeschatz-Abteilung 249, Russia 1942 Le Sturmgeschatz-Abteilung 249, créé le 10 janvier 1942, était le dernier des Sturmgeschatz-Abteilung initialement équipé de Sturmbeschatz armés du Stu.K L/24 7.5cm. On peut identifier le Ausf E par les nageoires plus longues des deux côtés de la superstructure. Les Sturmgeschatz Ausf. E du Sturmbeschatz-Abteilung 249 étaient peints en dunkelgrau RAL 7021 (gris foncé). Chaque Sturmgeschatz portait une lettre d'identification de chaque côté de la superstructure, à l'avant droit de la superstructure et sur la plaque arrière.

G Sturmgeschatz Aust. E, Sturmgeschatz-Abteilung 197, Russia 1942 Le Sturmgeschatz-Abteilung 197 créé le 25 novembre 1940 servit en Russie du sud. Comme c'est le cas de tous les blindés allemands de cette époque, il était peint en dunkelgrau RAL 7021 (gris foncé). Parmi les marquages, citons l'emblème Sturmbeschatz-Abteilung 197 'Kanoner Adler' (un aigle noir enserrant des grenades sur un bouclier blanc) à l'avant droit de la plaque de blindage supérieur du nez et sur le blindage arrière du diffuseur de fumée. Le 'Balkankreuz' était peint en noir et bordé de blanc.

wurde. Die 7,5cm-Versuchsgeschütze vom Typ Sturmkanone L/24 wurden von Krupp geliefert. Gepanzerter Fahrzeuge jener Periode waren mit unregelmäßigen Mustern in Tarnfarben versehen: RAL 7021 dunkelgrau, RAL 7017 dunkelbraun. Das ALR-Emblem war an den Kotflängern links vorne und rechts hinten zu sehen sowie an der Vorderplatte des Aufbaus neben der Sonnenblende des Fahrers. Diese fünf Fahrzeuge trugen einen Kennbuchstaben von A bis E links an der Aufbau-Vorderplatte. **A2** Sturmgeschütz Ausf. A (Fgst. Nr.90001-90030). 16. Sturmbatterie/Infanterieregiment "Großdeutschland" Die erste Einheit von Sturmgeschütz, Sturmbatterie 610, wurde im November 1939 gegründet, die das erste Sturmgeschütz Ausf.A von Daimler-Benz geliefert wurde.

B1 Sturmgeschütz Ausf. A (Fgst.Nr.90401-90420), Artillerie-Lehrregiment (ALR) in Jüterbog 1941 Im Juni und Juli 1940 wurde eine Serie von Sturmgeschütz-Fahrzeugen mit dem Fahrgestell von Pz.Kpfw. III Ausf.G hergestellt. Sie wurden ursprünglich an die Sturmbatterien 666 und 667 ausgegeben, kamen aber zu spät, um an der Invasion Frankreichs beteiligt zu sein. Einige dieser Ausf.A wurden vom ALR in Jüterbog als Ausbildungsfahrzeuge verwendet. An Juni 1940 waren deutsche Panzerfahrzeuge nur dunkelgrau (RAL 7021) gestrichen. **B2** Sturmgeschütz Ausf.B, Sturmgeschütz-Abteilung 192, Rußland 1941 Die Sturmgeschütz-Abteilung 192 wurde am 25. November 1940 gegründet; im April 1942 wurde die Abteilung in Sturmgeschütz-Abteilung "Großdeutschland" umbenannt. Die Sturmgeschütz-Fahrzeuge Ausf.B der Abteilung 192 waren dunkelgrau (RAL 7021) gestrichen.

C Sturmgeschütz Ausf.D, Fgst.Nr.90630, Sturmgeschütz-Abteilung 189, Rußland 1941 Am 9. Juli 1941 wurde die Sturmgeschütz-Abteilung 189 gegründet; sie erhielt eine Frist von vier Wochen bis zur Einsatzbereitschaft. Das Sturmgeschütz-Fahrzeug Ausf.D war im Juni 1941 von Alkeit fertiggestellt worden. Es war wie alle deutschen gepanzerten Fahrzeuge jener Periode dunkelgrau (RAL 7021) gestrichen. Zu den Markierungen gehören das "Ritter/Adler"-Emblem (kombiniertes Ritter-Adlerwappen) der Sturmgeschütz-Abteilung 189 am linken vorderen Kotflänger und an der hinteren Panzerung der Rauchkerzen-Ausgabe. Das Balkenkreuz war in einem weißen Umriß aufgemalt.

D Sturmgeschütz Ausf.B, Sturmgeschütz-Abteilung 191, Rußland 1941 Die Schnittzeichnung zeigt ein Sturmgeschütz-Fahrzeug Ausf.B, das an die im Oktober 1940 aufgestellte Sturmgeschütz-Abteilung 191 ausgegeben wurde. Es war dunkelgrau (RAL 7021) gestrichen; die Markierungen an beiden Aufbauseiten waren das weißumrissene Balkenkreuz und das Büffel-Emblem der Abteilung 191, das sich außerdem auch am Kotflänger vorne rechts sowie links vom Anlasserdeckel an der Heckplatte des Motorraums befand. Dieses Emblem zeigte einen roten Büffel auf einem schwarzen, rot eingefaßten Viereck.

E Sturmgeschütz Ausf.D, Sonderverband 288, Afrika 1942 Obwohl nur drei Sturmgeschütz-Fahrzeuge Ausf.D nach Nordafrikla geschickt wurden, sind sie doch allgemein bekannt, da das hier abgebildete Fahrzeug (Fgst.Nr.90683) nach der Erbeutung durch die britischen Streitkräfte gründlich untersucht und fotografiert wurde. Anfang 1942 wurde das Fahrzeug nach Afrika verschifft. Es war im Fronteinsatz in Bir Hacheim im Mai, in Acroma im Juni und in El Alamein im Oktober 1942. Für den Tropen-Einsatz wurden diese Fahrzeuge einem Befehl vom März 1941 zufolge neu gestrichen: in Gelbbraun (RAL 8000) und Graubraun (RAL 7008).

F Sturmgeschütz Ausf. E, Sturmgeschütz-Abteilung 249, Rußland 1942 Die Sturmgeschütz-Abteilung 249 , aufgestellt am 10. Januar 1942, war die letzte dieser Abteilungen, die von Anfang an mit Sturmgeschütz-Fahrzeugen ausgerüstet war, die über eine 7,5cm-Stu.K. L/24 verfügten. Die Version Ausf.E ist erkennbar durch die längeren Radgehäuse an beiden Seiten des Aufbaus; in der Abteilung 249 waren diese Fahrzeuge dunkelgrau (RAL 7021) gestrichen. Jedes der Fahrzeuge trug auch einen Kennbuchstaben an beiden Aufbauseiten, vorne rechts am Aufbau und an der Heckplatte.

G Sturmgeschütz Ausf. E, Sturmgeschütz-Abteilung 197, Rußland 1942 Die Sturmgeschütz-Abteilung 197 wurde am 25. November 1940 gegründet und war in Südrußland im Einsatz. Wie alle gepanzerten deutschen Fahrzeuge jener Periode waren auch diese dunkelgrau (RAL 7021) gestrichen. Markierungen waren das "Kanonen-Adler"-Emblem (ein schwarzer Adler mit Granaten in den Krallen auf einem weißen Schild) (vorne rechts oben auf der Panzerplatte und am Heck auf der Panzerung der Rauchkerzen-Ausgabe. Das Balkenkreuz war schwarz mit weißer Umrandung.